In praise of

R.I.S.E. After the Storm

"This is a great little book that is packed with many practical tips that can help business leaders make BIG changes to their life (both inside and outside of work) as well as learn how to run a business successfully. For those people who are not business leaders yet, this book will help you on a journey of self-discovery and assist you in achieving excellence in your work and in fulfilling your goals. The book is an easy read and one that you will want to carry around with you to refer to again and again."

– Dr. Robin Mann
Head – Centre for Organisational Excellence Research/
BPIR.com
Chairman, Global Benchmarking Network

"*R.I.S.E. After the Storm* provides a very practical guide to train and transform SMEs, especially during this Covid-19 pandemic. The R.I.S.E. framework offers proven techniques and principles to focus on people, process, and performance for sustainable success. It is easy to read and highly recommended."

– Simon Wong
Tzu Chi Merits Society Malaysia

"If you are looking to better your life and your business, read this book. *R.I.S.E. After the Storm* gives the business leader all the practical techniques to take their enterprise to the next level and achieve great results. It also provides very useful tips to achieve the right mindset to be a successful leader both in business and life. *R.I.S.E. After the Storm* is a well-worth easy read that I highly recommend!"

– Gisele Maxwell
Best-Selling Author of *Free and Wealthy Beyond Rich*

"Casey Ang's book is a gold mine of wisdom and practicality for any business owner. The R.I.S.E. principles and practices he shares pave the way for both personal and business growth, not only in times of challenge and change, but always. Do yourself and your business a favour: read this book, and implement Casey's advice!"

– **Annabelle Beckwith**
International business consultant and speaker
Author of *Get Your Peas in a Row: 5 key factors to propel your business forward*

"As a highly respected international business consultant, Casey brings two decades of practical business experience and wisdom to the written page. He has the knowledge and skills to identify productivity problems and turn challenges into opportunities. Casey understands that hard work alone will not bring success, so he teaches you how to set clear, intentional goals that will challenge and inspire you to elevate your thinking and begin to attract the results that you envision. *R.I.S.E. After the Storm* will transform your business as well as your personal life."

– **Darryl Bell**
Founder of Hope and Exchange
International Best-Selling Author of *We Are Creators*

"Sometimes it takes a while for us to realise that we have lost our way, and most times it takes even longer to recognise those who have the special ability to get us to believe in ourselves, to tie that belief to our highest ideals, and to find our way back to lead our business and our team towards great things.
The COVID-19 pandemic and its economic impact created a big need for this, as business leaders and SMEs alike instinctively flounder. With all the best tools and technology of our times, talents waiting for our nurturing and a disrupted market

waiting for us to capture, many of us are caught in the unexpected turmoil and need to figure out our way forward.

It isn't easy putting wisdom into concise and easy words, but this book does just that – it reminds us of the time we started our business and why we did it, it rejuvenates the fight and the enterprise spirit, it gives us clarity, and it inspires us to dig deep find our direction and reach for what we know is possible. To my fellow SMEs, evolve and emerge triumphant after the storm! This book will get you started."

– Datin Lorela Chia
Central Chairman, Small & Medium Enterprises Association (SAMENTA) Malaysia

R.I.S.E.
AFTER THE STORM

EVOLVE YOUR MINDSET
FOR BUSINESS EXCELLENCE

CASEY ANG

Published by
Hasmark Publishing
www.hasmarkpublishing.com

Permission should be addressed in writing to
caseyang@casey-ang.com

Editor: Kathryn Young
kathryn@hasmarkpublishing.com

Cover & Book Design: Anne Karklins
anne@hasmarkpublishing.com

ISBN 13: 978-1-989756-43-0
ISBN 10: 1989756433

In memory of
my beloved father Ang Hock Ho

DEDICATION

My Parents, Ang Hock Ho and Ong Gaik Lian

To my parents, who have loved me and supported me all these years, I deeply appreciate all the sacrifices and hard work you have put in for us. Thank you from the bottom of my heart. I am so grateful and proud to be your son. I love you.

My Wife, Jessica Dang

This book is specially dedicated to my dear wife: your unconditional support and love are the pillars of strength that keep me moving. A simple thank you is not enough to tell you how much I appreciate you being there for me rain or shine. Thank you for supporting me in doing what I do best. I am so grateful to have you as my better half. I love you.

My Sons, Wei Sheng and Wei Jun

To my dear sons, I want you to know that you are my inspiration and the sunshine of my life. I want you to know that you have unlimited potential, so go all out to live your life to the fullest. Be empowered in your life. Live your life with full faith, loving, and caring. I am proud of you. I love you.

My Daughters, Li Shie and Amber

Thank you for coming into our family. Your presence means a lot to my wife and me. Even though we have no blood relation, your willingness to come into our family and call us "papa and mama" makes our life more complete and brings joy and happiness to our family. Be empowered in your life. Live your life to the fullest with full faith, loving, and caring. I am proud of you. I love you.

TABLE OF CONTENTS

INTRODUCTION

In creating the R.I.S.E. Mindset™ framework, I've drawn on my twenty years of experience to share with small- to medium-sized enterprises (SMEs) simple ways to ensure their business not only survives this challenging period but that it also rises to become more effective than ever.

With challenging problems come opportunities. You can choose to react during a crisis period and feel stressed, worried, and depressed, OR you can choose to respond by stepping back, reflecting, and identifying how to create greater value for your customers and your community. Well-planned actions not only enable you to weather a crisis but also empower your business and you to rise higher.

Figure 1.1 Be As Strong As the Flexible and Resilient Reed

Are you feeling daunted? Consider the humble reed you might see in a pond or a stream. No matter how strong a storm is, a reed will never break. When a storm comes, the wind blows, the reed bends, and, when the storm is over, the reed rises again. Where a huge tree might topple in a storm, the humble reed is flexible and strong.

I have one simple goal in writing this book, which is *to train and transform SMEs during this very critical period of global pandemic caused by COVID-19.* My sincere and humble message is that SMEs can be just as strong as the flexible and resilient reed, and once this storm of COVID-19 is over, you can RISE even higher.

The book is divided into four sections:

Raise Your Awareness

Inside Out

Set Clear Goals

Engage and Excel

Raise Your Awareness. These chapters provide techniques to understand better the sweet spots in your organization and how you can leverage them to accelerate recovery and grow your business. You also will learn why raising awareness of your *true self* can help you master techniques to tap into the unlimited potential hiding deep inside you.

How can becoming more aware of your true potential help your business not only recover but perform better? Well, businesses are operated and managed by people. If the people who run and manage a business don't understand their full potential, no amount of training and tools will make a differ-ence. Until you gain *clarity* about yourself, you won't be able to turn the challenges in front of you into opportunities.

Once you gain awareness of your true potential, we'll discuss how to identify the sweet spots in your business that can, with conscious effort, yield greater productivity, reduce unnecessary waste (which is crucial for every organization), and double your business's output.

Inside Out. Rather than focus on external factors beyond your control at this crucial time, it's essential to look inward. This section guides you through the process of discovering your unique individual and organizational strengths and determining how these strengths can help you transform your business into a gold mine. We'll talk about the principles of *giving and taking* along with *cause and effect.* You will learn that you can effectively shape your outside world if you're properly attuned to your inside world. This applies not only to your personal life but to your business! At the business level, too often we focus on output, forgetting that output is directly related to input and how we turn the input into the output. In this section, I will show you the techniques to hone your process so that it consistently gives you the output you want and need, especially at this time of economic turbulence.

Set Clear Goals. When you set your intention, you're better able to focus your energy to support your aims. Crystal-clear intentions enable a transformation process through which you can turn ideas into reality. Too often, we focus on *what we do not want* but end up somehow getting more of it. Why? Well, energy will go wherever you focus your attention. If you keep focusing on what you don't want, what you worry about, you are going to attract more of that into your life. STOP focusing on what you don't want and START focusing on what you do want! The objective of this section is to guide you through the process of setting a goal. *Why do I need to learn how to set a clear goal?* you might be thinking. Setting a goal sounds simple, and it is simple. The challenge is in shifting the paradigm in your mind to be able to set a goal that will inspire you, energize you, and propel you into taking action that will bring you closer to achieving the goal. In this section, I will share with you the techniques and questions you should ask yourself when setting a goal as well as how to set a goal that achieves results you want. The techniques I share here will apply to your personal goals as well as your business goals.

Engage and Excel. Doing something halfheartedly inevitably leads not to excellence but to half-cooked results! Every one of us has twenty-four hours in the day, and each day we spend eight or nine hours at work. Business results and individual performance are directly related to how you allocate your time. In this section, we'll take a closer look at where you spend your energy. How can you and your team avoid spending energy in a wasteful way? We'll discuss how you can leverage your team members' inner strengths to address problematic business practices that cause unnecessary follow-up, delays, or wait times between processes. I will also share with you technology solutions you can leverage to digitalize your processes so that your team can focus fully on adding value to activities rather than chasing information, arguing, or debating why important steps have been overlooked. We'll also discuss technologies that can help measure your team's performance in real time so that they can fully engage and excel at their work.

As I wrote this book, I visualized the many SMEs, and the dedicated people behind them, that have the power to RISE, even in the midst of the current crisis. If you commit to mastering the techniques I share in this book, someday soon I know we will toast to your success—and more importantly, to the joy of discovering your true self and the higher purpose of your life.

Enjoy the journey of learning. When you master these strategies, the sky is the limit. You'll be unstoppable.

To your success!

RAISE
YOUR
AWARENESS

CHAPTER 1

GAIN CLARITY

Until you gain clarity about your true self,
you are not performing at your fullest potential.
– Casey Ang

Let's imagine you had a time machine that could take you back to the moment you were born. Let's also imagine you had a device that could help you understand your newborn mindset. There you are, full of potential. Nothing is impossible. Your heart is overflowing with curiosity. You long to explore and find out more about what you can do. You have no fear, no worries about how people look at or think about you. In fact, it is in that state of mind that you learn how to walk and talk, along with many other skills you develop in the early stages of your life. But as you grow up, you start to get comments, feedback, and suggestions; some are positive and constructive; some are negative and destructive. You start to realize what you can and cannot do, and you start to believe you are capable of some things and not capable of others, based on what the people around you tell you. Eventually, you form a strong belief— a paradigm—about you and your capabilities.

How has this affected your life so far? Have you ever stopped pursuing a goal you once set because your inner voice somehow told you that you were not capable of achieving it? Have you ever encountered a situation where you were in the middle of some discussion, and you wanted to express your point of view, and the words came to your lips, yet you decided just to keep quiet? Why? Perhaps you've thought of a new idea or imagined a solution to a problem, but before you put any effort into it, you stop because you just sense somehow that it won't work out. I could go on, but I think you understand my point, don't you?

Your Thinking Affects Your Actions and Hence Your Results

The results you are getting today are directly related to the actions you have taken in the past. Here are a couple of wise sayings about the connection between your thinking and your results:

If you always do what you always did, you will always get what you always got.
Insanity: doing the same thing over and over again and expecting different results.

To put it in a slightly different way, to change your results, you need to change your actions!

The challenge here is that most of the time your actions are driven less by observations than by feelings. We let situations, people, and circumstances influence what we do. Your feelings play a huge role in determining your actions and thus determine your results.

So, what impacts your feelings? You see, we have five knowledge-acquiring senses that affect how we think and feel. These five senses enable us to see, hear, smell, taste, and touch. Based on what we are seeing, hearing, smelling, tasting, and touching, we derive an emotional feeling toward certain objects, people, situations, and circumstances. We respond to emotional feelings by reacting. For example, if you sense danger, you react by running away. If you sense risk, you may refrain from taking further steps or become doubtful and indecisive.

If you always allow objects, people, situations, and circumstances to affect your feelings and thus your actions, then you are letting external circumstances dictate your sense of confidence—and possibly your life! Someone whose feelings are easily affected by what people say or do is like a marionette. It's time to regain control by putting a stop to this emotional response. Because if you don't learn how to take control of this cycle, then your mind will be in a state of restlessness, like a monkey jumping from one branch to another. Think about this: if you are in this restlessness state of mind in our current challenging situation, how are you going to understand your business's needs with any clarity? How can you devise a creative solution to help your company weather the economic turbulence caused by the COVID-19 pandemic?

Especially at a time like now, you need to be able to distinguish between what's happening in your external environment and what your business actually needs. If you don't, then chances are you will experience fear, worry, and stress most of the time.

To make this distinction, you need to find a way to reconnect to your true self. How?

Five Major Hindrances

Consider the five major hindrances preventing you from connecting to your true self. These five hindrances cover up your true potential, like a cloud covers up the sun on a rainy day. The five hindrances are *greed, hatred, ignorance, ego,* and *doubt.*

Greed is like a hole without a bottom. A person who is in this state of mind can't find inner peace because they're always chasing after something, always in a scarcity mindset. In this person's mind, resources and wealth are limited, so they might say, "I need to grasp as much as I can" or "If I give away or share what I have with other people, then I am going to have less." This person thinks about their own bottom line and never about what they can do to help others or how they can add value to others.

Hatred is another dangerous hindrance that you need to be aware of. Someone who is in this state of mind can easily get agitated by people and circumstances. When the external environment is not congruent with someone's expectations, someone hindered by hatred might become emotional and enraged. Often, anger inhibits his ability to see or understand the truth of what is happening. His energy is spent in a wasteful way, blaming everything and everyone but himself for his problems. People do not like to work closely with this type of person; if they do so, most likely, it is because this person is in a position of authority.

Ignorance, or *avidya* in Vedic Sanskrit, means having a wrong understanding of the nature of reality. Consider that nothing is permanent. A new car will get old, or a person you love may not permanently stay with you—there will always be ups and downs in every aspect of your life. Even this body you are living in is not permanent. This body is not the real you. There is a spirit living inside this temporary body; one day, this body will decay, and eventually, the spirit will leave and move into another body. Gaining awareness about this fundamental truth is crucial because it helps you to realize that you are not your body, not your mind, and not your feelings! When you make this mental shift, your inner self—your true self—will start taking charge, and you'll stop letting people, situations, and external circumstances have control over you.

The fourth hindrance is *ego*, which is the illusion of the self. People who are driven by their ego have a very strong affinity to "my, me, mine," and they fail to realize the truth of nature: nothing is permanent. Ego-driven behavior is often related to something impermanent, such as status or title. Therefore, someone in this state of mind always feels fear, worry, and stress and wastes energy trying to defend their point of view or status.

Finally, there is *doubt*. When someone is in this state of mind, they get stuck—nothing gets done. They become indecisive and waste a lot of time without moving forward because of fear. Doubt also reflects a person's failure to understand the nature of abundance. Doubt about one's own capabilities and potential obscures the fact of our unlimited potential. People in this state of mind lack energy and passion in their work. Instead of thinking about how to make things happen, they worry, "What if this or that happens?" or "What if things don't work out as I've planned?" or "What will other people say about me?" And so on.

Stay in the State of Your True Potential

The main objective of this chapter is to help you gain clarity about your true self, your true potential. In doing so, you will raise your awareness about the real you living inside this temporary body. You will realize that you are not your body, your mind, or your feelings. You will become immune to criticism and to what happens externally. You'll take note and become aware of what is happening in your environment, but you won't allow it to steer you away from achieving your goals, from doing what you want to do.

Once you embrace your unlimited potential, you won't have any doubts about your capabilities. Instead of saying, "I don't know," you'll start to say, "I have not learned how to do this yet, and if I need that skill, I am going to learn it." Nothing can stop you when you are in this state of mind, including the current economic challenges. Because now you realize and understand that nothing is permanent, and this, too, shall pass in time. You know and believe that you can weather this crisis. Therefore, instead of worrying, you will use your energy to think about how you can add value for your customers and how you can help more people solve their problems.

You'll start to get closer to your true self. You'll understand your unlimited potential, yet you'll stay humble and respect the people around you. You'll bond with people, and they'll enjoy working with you. Doing so will allow you to get more things done.

You'll start to take control of your own life. Your mind will settle down, and you can feel the peace inside you. You'll watch every thought that arises in your mind, and once you notice the five hindrances, they won't be hindrances to you anymore. You'll take full responsibility for the results you are getting and spend your energy figuring out solutions. Creative ideas will start surfacing one by one, and you will know you are making positive progress every day toward your goals.

You'll become bigger than your problem! You'll seek solutions and solve problems and challenges. You'll solve problems bit by bit instead of being controlled by the problems. You'll understand that behind every challenging problem, there are many opportunities.

I encourage you to read this section every day for the next thirty days. Let this beautiful truth settle into your subconscious. Let it become the foundation of your new belief system—the new you!

How to Regain Clarity

Here are three key ways to connect with your true self and weaken those destructive hindrances.

Spend time in silence each day. Give yourself at least thirty minutes in the morning and at night just to be with yourself quietly. If thirty minutes is too difficult at first, do this for five to ten minutes and then gradually work your way up to thirty minutes. Trust me, this time that you spend with yourself is worth it. You have twenty-four hours in a day, so I think it isn't too much to give just five, ten, or thirty minutes to yourself in the morning and at night. Find a quiet place and eliminate distractions. Put your phone on silent. Just sit, relax, listen, and observe your breathing in and out. Watch the thoughts that surface in your mind, but don't follow them. Just observe the thoughts that arise and notice them. Focus on breathing and relax. If you have the opportunity to learn meditation, go for it. Practicing silent moments daily allows you to get closer to your true self.

Be in the present moment. Practice allowing your mind to stay in the present moment. The past is gone, the future is unknown, so focus on doing what you can do now; it is the most precious gift you can give to yourself. Instead of wasting your energy worrying about the future or feeling regret and shame about what has already happened in the past, channel all your energy into the present moment. Pay full attention to every conversation you have and what you're doing in each moment. This focus not only helps to improve your relationships but also helps improve your productivity and effectiveness.

Become more aware of the fact that you are not your body, your mind, or your feelings. Watch the five hindrances when you notice them occurring in your life and take charge of them. Do not allow people and situations to influence your emotions and your actions. Know that there is a true you, a pure spirit living inside this temporary body. Get closer to your true self. You will come to realize that your thinking affects your feelings, and your feelings affect your actions.

Summary

Here are the key points from this chapter:

- You have unlimited potential. Start to take control of your life and stop letting the people, situations, and circumstances around you dictate what you can achieve in your life.

- Practice silent moments daily.

- Live your life moment by moment and focus your mind and energy into carrying out the actions that will bring you closer to your goals.

- Step into the field of uncertainty and enjoy the process of discovering all the possibilities.

- Live your life in an abundant way.

CHAPTER 2

FOCUS ON THE SWEET SPOTS IN YOUR BUSINESS

*It is not a matter of how to do something;
it is a matter of what to do.*
– Casey Ang

When it comes to thinking about how to improve your business's performance, you need to begin by understanding where and what to improve. Because if you know the what, then the how becomes clear automatically. This understanding is especially true right now during the pandemic. You need to be able to plan your resources well and work on the right things.

As the world starts to recover and come out of this pandemic, organizations will start getting back to work. Businesses will gradually recover, some sooner than others; some may not even make it. But how can you make sure your business weathers this pandemic and the subsequent recovery period? Where and what should you focus on? How will you deal with a backlog of work? How will you cope with your customers' revised expectations as they, too, work to deal with their backlog? How are you going to face global supply chain shortages? If you aren't clear about the answers to these questions, chances are you may hit the panic button when the time comes. My experience tells me you may not be able to bring your business back to normal fast enough if you attempt to target the entire organization. You need to focus on some sweet spots! This concept is what we'll discuss in this chapter.

There are five important components to focus on: Visibility, Traceability, Connectivity, Productivity, and Capability (VT-CPC). I call these the sweet spots because you'll learn just how sweet they are if you get them right, whether you're in manufacturing, trading, or the service industry. They matter to businesses of all kinds.

Visibility

If you walk into your office or onto your manufacturing floor, are you able to tell immediately whether things are on the right track? Are you able to spot whether a project got stuck somewhere, and why? As you travel to generate new business, are you able to log into your company intranet and immediately see whether the internal operations are going smoothly? These are all critical questions for you as an owner, founder, or senior manager of your company.

Running a business without a clear visual dashboard to indicate how healthy the business is, how operations are going, and whether there are any critical issues is like a pilot flying without knowing whether the engines are functioning, whether the fuel is sufficient, and at what altitude the plane is flying. (In chapter 8, I will share with you some simple, cost-effective technology that can help you establish an effective digital dashboard.)

Yet, as a business consultant who focuses on helping organizations accelerate their business performance, I often see this happen! It sometimes comes as a surprise when I have a factory tour. During my very first visit, together with the senior management, the people on site can't even tell me yesterday's output, the status of projects in progress, or other key information.

Visibility is essential. Without it, a business constantly will be in the position of putting out fires rather than preventing them from happening in the first place. Why? Well, going back to the factory example, people only realize that they can't meet a planned delivery when they're able to see it in conjunction with the shipping date. People only realize the potential for a bottleneck when they can anticipate backlogs. So many basic business problems can be avoided with the help of visibility, so establish systems to support it.

There are three major and obvious benefits you can gain from establishing clear visibility of your business's operations and performance.

First, clear visibility allows you and your team to spot bottlenecks in your company's workflow and to act on them quickly before it's too late. You and your team can also provide more accurate updates to the customers, for example, with delivery dates. With clear visibility around work status, you and your team will be better able to plan how you allocate resources to ensure a smooth workflow from beginning to end.

Second, by creating a dashboard that shows who is doing what at any given time, you can instill greater responsibility and accountability among your team members. With a tool like this in place, people cannot hide problems from you.

Finally, as legendary management consultant Peter Drucker said, "What gets measured gets done." Where the attention goes, the energy flows. By establishing a clear dashboard that helps visualize performance around some key indicators, as shown in figure 2.1, people get to see how they are performing in real time. They get to see how they can influence the indicator shown on the dashboard. For example, by clearing a backlog, they can make the backlog indicator turn green! If done well, a tool like this can boost the overall morale of the whole team.

This doesn't mean you should put everything into the dashboard and start tracking and measuring every single detail of your business and operations. You need to carefully select and design what you want to make visible and measure. Because what you measure may influence people's behavior. Here are some important points for you to consider when establishing a visual dashboard:

- At what critical points in your processes will delays jeopardize the ability to fulfill a customer's order on time? (We'll discuss more about this in chapter 4.)

- Do you have an effective method or gateway to collect real-time data at these critical points?

- Who in your organization needs to monitor what, and how frequently do they need to monitor it?

- What actions can people take after seeing the dashboard? You need to make sure people who are watching this dashboard know what they should do based on the indicator shown there. It is a waste of energy and effort if people do not know what they should do based on the indicator shown.

- What behavior changes are you expecting by using the dashboard with your team?

- Remember, when it comes to designing a visual dashboard, less is more.

Figure 2.1 Example of Digital Dashboard

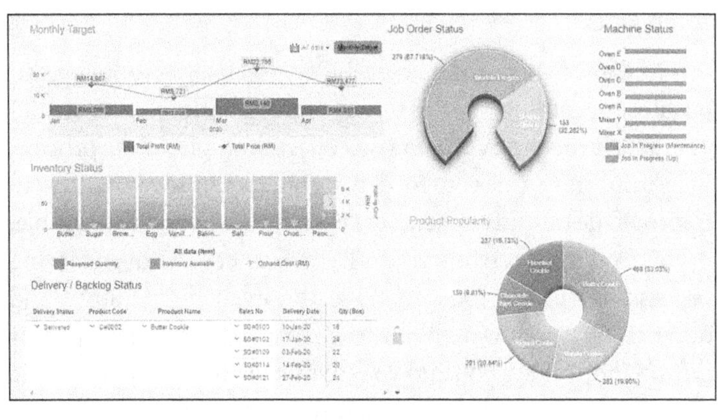

Traceability

The International Organization of Standardization (ISO) defines traceability as "the ability to trace the history, application, use, and location of an item or its characteristics through record identification data."

In layman's terms, traceability means you can trace and track finished goods or products through the whole supply chain, from origin to destination and vice versa. When required, you can provide information on what materials the products are made of and the data that is captured in the process of producing them.

Traceability is another important sweet spot to focus on. It is not just because this is a requirement of ISO 9001 certification, but more importantly, because of the benefits your organization can gain from it.

To achieve good traceability, you need to be able to identify finished goods, semi-finished goods, works in progress, and raw material. Clear identification helps you to assess the status of a lot/project in the operations area. As such, a good practice of clear identification and traceability can help you to prevent many unnecessary issues, such as faulty processes, defective or incorrect parts, and other missteps that can lead to customer complaints.

On top of that, good traceability practices also help your business in gaining a better understanding of the characteristics of critical processes via data you collect throughout the process. It is important for you to drive quality improvement or to improve the output capacity of certain processes. For example, if you find a defective part and you suspect the oven-drying process caused it, you can trace the oven temperature and other settings that were in place when a lot was produced. This information allows you and your team to identify whether there were any abnormalities when producing that lot. Another example: in the order-processing process, with clear identification and traceability, you're able to know what types of orders take a long time for your team to complete. This metric would help you allocate resources and make adjustments to how that type of order is processed. This knowledge can help to shorten the cycle time and increase the output.

Here are some important points for you to consider when setting up helpful traceability and identification metrics in your business operation:

- What are the important work statuses in each process that need to be identified to prevent mixing up lots/projects that have different statuses?

- How are you going to trace and record the important information or data throughout the process of completing the project or producing the finished goods?

- How easy and how fast can you trace and furnish the relevant information for goods/projects when required?

- What is the purpose of tracking those data or information? How are you going to make use of them to drive improvement?

- Is there a simple and obvious way to identify the status and location (and more) of a work in progress (WIP) so that people can easily tell in one second where the WIP is in the process?

- Have you explored cost-effective technology that can help you to do a better job with traceability and identification?

Connectivity

It doesn't matter whether you are a manufacturer, a wholesaler, a restaurant owner, a retailer, or a service provider, you need well-connected processes to provide excellent service to your customers. As a business owner, you might tend to focus on the outcome, the output, the revenue, the profits. There's nothing wrong with that, and in fact, you need to know and be aware of this. However, the point I want to make is that those outputs, revenue, and profits come from the work processes in your company. A *well-designed and connected process* will yield higher output, giving you higher revenue and profits. On the other hand, a poorly designed and disconnected process will cause unnecessary wait times and delays. This type of process will cause inefficiency and an increase in headcounts and costs, which may badly affect the revenue and profits of your business in the long run.

Do not underestimate the importance of well-connected processes. Invest some time and effort into getting it right. I know designing a well-connected process can be tedious and requires a huge amount of time and resources initially. But if you compare this proactive effort to the effort you put into chasing orders/work/projects and the number of times your customers have been disappointed because you fail to deliver or fail to complete your project on time—which is more worthwhile? I think you know the answer, don't you?

I often see businesses, particularly SMEs, caught in the dilemma of getting more business and orders in and then struggling to fulfill those orders. As a result, I can see senior management and the founders of these SMEs spending more time making sure operations run well rather than with their customers, all the while continuing to court more business. What is going wrong here? On the one hand, you need to grow your business by developing more customers and getting more orders, but meanwhile, you, as the owner of the company, are being sucked into its operations. Therefore, you don't have time to meet more customers and develop more business!

What is the meaning of *connectivity*? It means all the work can flow from the beginning to the end seamlessly, without unnecessary stoppage due to waiting for information or materials. People running the process understand one another's expectations of the process; they know what to provide and when to provide it. They know how much time they have to complete the tasks at hand. They know the level of quality they are responsible for delivering. You do not need someone to remind them; they just know what they need to do, when they need to do it, how fast they must complete a task, and who is next in the process after them. Imagine, if you have a well-designed and connected process in place in your organization, what will your customers' experience be like? How much more business can you bring in then?

Sometimes I encounter SMEs that think if they put sophisticated software like Enterprise Resource Planning (ERP) in place, they've automatically connected their process. This isn't true! Getting an ERP vendor to digitalize your current process doesn't mean you have a well-connected process in place. It simply means you've moved your current process to a digital platform. Chances are you just complicated the process, and to a certain extent, you've enabled your people to serve the technology (in this case, ERP software), rather than enabling the technology to serve the people! I've seen people put so many data fields and unnecessary steps into the ERP and spend money getting the ERP vendor to do lots of customization because they want the process to run how it was ten years ago—or since day one!

The point is, just because something has been done a certain way since day one does not necessarily mean that it is a good process. Instead of simply moving a less-than-adequate process online, like many SMEs or sometimes even some multi-national corporations (MNCs) do, you need to know that creating a well-connected process or digitalizing your process via ERP means simplifying it. If you can get things done in just one step or one click, you do not want to put in a process that requires three or five steps—even if that's the way you have been doing it since day one!

We'll discuss more about how to create well-designed and connected processes in chapter 4.

Productivity

In challenging times like this, increasing productivity is not a choice—it is a MUST! Failure to do so can cause negative impacts to a business, such as delays in work, increases in resources, and rises in costs.

The days of just working hard are gone. You need to make sure that your team is not only working hard but working smart. Productivity refers to the ability to produce greater output with the same or less input. In other words, do less and achieve more!

There are a few ways for us to look at how to raise productivity at work. Let's discuss some of the important and most prominent ones based on my consultation experience.

First, are people using the right tool to do the work? Whenever I am given a task to improve the productivity of a certain work process, I always check whether people working on the process are given the right tool to perform their work. For example, have we provided the workers who are doing the assembly work the right jigs and fixtures? Are they using the right Allen key to tighten the parts together, or must they always search for the Allen key because it is being shared among all the technicians who are doing the same job? Is the person who has the responsibility of performing data analysis given the right computer with the appropriate tools to cope with the amount of data they have to deal with? This issue is so fundamental, and yet I still see businesses that do not pay attention to simple and fundamental things when it comes to analyzing productivity.

Second, productivity is about the ability to do the right thing rather than just doing things correctly. We can do a hundred things correctly, but out of those, only 20 percent may be the right thing that gets the work completed. What do I mean by this? As we discussed in the Connectivity section, a poorly designed and disconnected process can cause people to perform lots of unnecessary tasks or steps. In a lean manufacturing concept, these are commonly referred to as non-value-added activities. As such, to improve the productivity in your company, you need to make sure the end-to-end processes are well designed and connected.

Third, you need to find a way to minimize unnecessary information seeking. How often do your people stop their work because they don't have the information they require when they need it? Have you seen a lot of emails flying back and forth as people pursue the information or data required in between processes? Failing to fix this issue can cause lots of unnecessary waiting times and delays in production.

Finally, how many reports and how much data on a daily, weekly, or monthly basis is important and required? Are there any redundant reports being produced by two or more departments or people in your organization? This redundancy is another important aspect you need to examine in your company to raise productivity. Sometimes, I see managers and supervisors sitting in front of computers for hours crunching data for reports that have little value or reports that can be simplified and automated in just a few clicks. Instead of spending hours in front of computers trying to crunch data or generate reports, they should be spending time understanding the challenges in the processes, finding ways to shorten the cycle time, or even looking into how to improve the capability of the people and process.

Here are some tips to improve productivity in your business:

- Check whether people are given the right tools to perform their tasks.

- Follow what we discuss in chapter 4 to align processes, simplify them, and remove unnecessary steps and bureaucracy from the process.

- Scrutinize information and data required by each process, and make sure the information and data are available when needed.

- Find ways to simplify data crunching and the reporting process and avoid redundant and repetitive reports and data entry.

- Visibility, Traceability, Connectivity, and Capability can all impact Productivity. Make sure you get them right.

Capability

When is the last time you reviewed the capability of your people and machines and checked whether they still align with your current business model? Are they up to date based on the latest technology and developments in your industry? Do you have a comprehensive one-to-three-year capability development plan in place?

I'm always surprised and worried when I see a company that doesn't invest in raising their employees' capability. To a certain extent, some companies leave this to individuals within the company. In other words, they let it happen more or less by chance. I know that can sound a bit harsh. I highlight this with the intention of raising your awareness about how important it is for you to establish a comprehensive plan to develop the capabilities that align with your business strategies and directions.

You need to look at the six aspects of capability, as shown in figure 2.2, and build your strengths around them.

Figure 2.2 The Six Capability Strengths

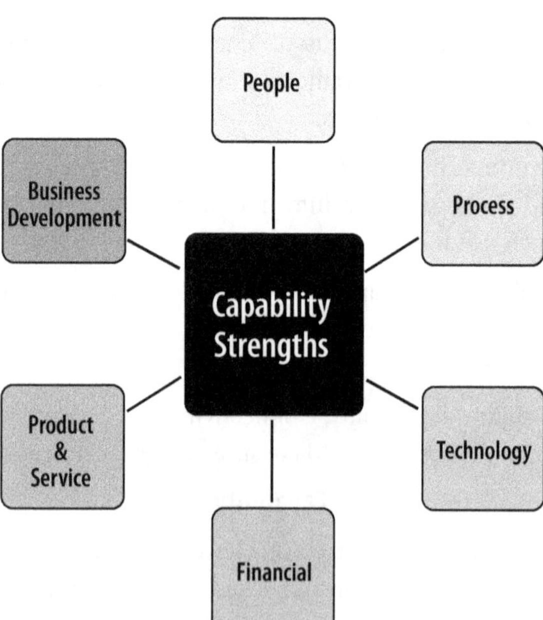

People

People are your company's greatest asset. You need to develop a solid plan to continuously assess the capabilities of your people and put efforts into improving them. What new knowledge, skills, and experiences do your people need to have to align with your business strategy and direction? What kind of soft skills and technical skills training do your people require? What kind of exposure must your key team have to gain the experience they need? How can you put in place a mentoring, coaching, or buddy system to improve the team capability that aligns with your business requirements?

Process

Are your company's processes capable of meeting customer and market requirements? Are the processes running at a speed that allows you to cope with current demands and future growth? You may have processes that work well when your business is running at a smaller scale, but as your business grows, if you don't put effort into raising process capability, you will soon realize that the process you have had in place since day one is no longer sustainable.

For example, when your company is operating around or below USD5Mil to USD10Mil in revenue, you may not have a proper job-order issuing system or even an inventory control system. The latter enables people to see what is happening, how much inventory is available, and whether the inventory is adequate. But as your business grows to USD100Mil and above, your existing processes can no longer support it. As the volume of transactions increases, and if you do nothing to improve your process capability, your systems will break down, and as a result, your headcount or costs might rise.

Technology

Is the technology you are deploying capable of meeting the requirements of the market? Have you explored cost-effective technology you can leverage to accelerate the performance of your business? How much of the process technology you have in place is actually being used by your team? Is the technology you have in place serving the process and people well, or is it in the way? (We'll talk more about this in chapter 8.)

Financial

What have you done to build your financial strength to support your business's expansion and anticipate economic challenges like we are facing now? Do you know what your profit drivers and cost contributors are? When it comes to improving operational performance, I believe we should tie it back to the impact on *financial* performance. This approach enables the operations team to identify the right things to focus on. This is the reason I am equipping my consulting company with a team of finance experts to work closely with operational improvement experts.

Products and Services

How strong and innovative are your products and services? Are they aligned with the demands from customers and consumers in the markets? Having a clear product and service roadmap is so crucial, and it is an important capability that you need to build up. How fast is your current time to market for new products? When have you "missed the boat" on some of these aspects? Did your product development team focus on manufacturability (meaning the product is easy to manufacture)? Or did they focus on marketability (meaning the ability of a product to be sold in the market)? Do your business development and sales teams align with the company product roadmap?

Business Development

The best products need to be backed by solid business development strategies and execution. Never hope for "build a better mousetrap, and the world will beat a path to your door!" You need to focus on developing the capabilities of your business development team to help them reach the markets, widen your reach, and penetrate new territory. You need to be innovative in terms of how you are going to reach your customers. Track your quotation conversion rate and work on a way to improve it. How can you be more innovative to generate more new leads for your business?

Summary

Your willingness and commitment to focus energetically on all five of the sweet spots (VT-CPC) will enable you to create a strong foundation that allows you to weather this crisis or any crisis. I believe if you do VT-CPC right, it will improve your business's effectiveness and efficiency by at least two times. When the storm is over, your business will be ready to RISE to new heights.

INSIDE
OUT

CHAPTER 3

BE THE MASTER OF YOUR LIFE

You do not know what you are capable of achieving
until you actually do it.
– Casey Ang

By now, we have discussed gaining clarity about your true potential as well as identifying and strengthening the five sweet spots (VT-CPC) in your business. In this chapter, we are going to discuss how you can learn to be the master of your own life. This is so crucial because people who cannot master their own minds will have difficulty in managing their business and career.

About fifteen years ago, I attended a live three-day seminar by T. Harv Eker, the author of *Secrets of the Millionaire Mind*, in Singapore. In the seminar, there was a phrase the speaker said that shook me: "Your inner world creates your outer world." And I love what the author mentioned in *Secrets of the Millionaire Mind* that "It is not enough to be in the right place at the right time. You have to be the right person in the right place at the right time."

When it comes to mindset—like attracts like. If you live in a state of worry, fear, and stress, then you are going to attract more of the same. What goes out into the universe energetically comes back! So, when what you've worried about actually happens, and you keep asking, "Why is this happening to me?" well, what is going on inside your mind has found a way to manifest in your outer world. On the flip side, the world's greatest inventions—airplanes, satellites, smartphones—all appeared first in the minds of their inventors. Having said that, I think it's important to recognize that not all crises or negative events (COVID-19, for example) are manifestations of people's worries and fears. In facing a big crisis like our current one, focus your mind on what you want instead of what you do not want.

The point that I would like to emphasize here is that the outcomes you are getting today result from the actions you took in the past. You created where you are today! If you like what you are, what you see now in your life, keep doing what you've been doing. And vice versa, if you don't like where you are now or the results you are achieving in your life, career, and business, then you have to change your actions. Remember:

If you always do what you always did, you will always get what you always got.
Insanity: doing the same thing over and over again and expecting different results.

If you understand what I explained in the first two chapters and what I am about to share with you in this chapter, you can take charge of your life. You can empower yourself by practicing the following simple and yet powerful principles of Giving, Gratitude, and Cause and Effect.

Giving

I am sure you've heard, "The more you give, the more you get." Someone who abides by this principle understands how nature works. What happens if the water in the drain stops flowing? It stinks! You see, exchange must be constant. Money, blood, energy—it all has to keep circulating for systems to remain healthy. Consider the exchange of oxygen and carbon dioxide between humans and plants, and the fact that *chi* or energy in a person's body must flow for us to remain healthy.

Start cultivating an abundance mindset! Tell yourself that there is always enough for you to share with the people around you. Practice giving something to everyone you come into contact with. It can be as simple as a smile. It can be a sincere compliment you give to someone who did a good job. It can be the change you get after paying your bill that you put into a donation box. Or it can even be a simple, silent prayer in your heart for others.

In the office where you work, practicing giving can also mean giving 100 percent of your attention to colleagues who are presenting or talking something over with you. It means putting in your best efforts in completing your tasks and sharing your knowledge and experiences with your colleagues. It means giving your sincere compliments to your team members who did a good job.

Practice giving and sharing with pure intention. Pure intention means you give and share with no expectations of reciprocity. You just give with the intention of helping other people and creating more happiness for the people around you. As you practice this, you will notice the peace and happiness within you. To me, this is something money can't buy. What about you?

A long-lasting relationship between people must be based on the principle of giving and sharing. No one is willing to work with someone who always focuses on "me, my, mine!" Instead, the person who always focuses on "What can I do to add value for people? How can I help more people around me to be happier and more successful?" will be able to build a good rapport with people—and people will like to work with this kind of person.

Gratitude

Next, we should cultivate a gratitude mindset. Express your sincere gratitude to all the things, people, situations, opportunities, and challenges that come into your life. Learn to appreciate everything you have now. You know, sometimes, we tend to take things for granted and forget to express our appreciation toward what we are receiving or have. Even a bowl of white rice contains the contribution of so many people—the farmers, the manufacturer who processed it, the logistics provider who distributed it, the retailer who sold it to us, the rice cooker manufacturer that provided us with equipment to cook the rice, and so on.

Learn to receive all things that come to you with an open heart and with full gratitude. If someone praises you because you did a good job, say *thank you.* If your customer challenges you to improve your delivery performance, say *thank you.* Everything happens and comes to you for a reason. Opportunities like to hide behind problems and challenges. If you learn to accept things happening to you with a gratitude mindset, you are always in control. When good things happen, you express your appreciation, and you work even harder to enhance further what you have done well. When bad times come, you accept those times with gratitude, knowing there is something for you to learn.

If a person is always in a gratitude mindset, then nothing can stop this person. In good times, this person will remain humble and continue to share and help more people. In bad times, this person just accepts things as they are, appreciates the opportunities for learning and growth, and focuses on what they can do to overcome challenges. Instead of blaming other people, or the situations and circumstances, the person who has a gratitude mindset is always able to reflect and learn from issues or challenges and eventually comes back even stronger.

Remember this: the more you are grateful, the more you are going to attract good things toward you to be thankful for. Get yourself a gratitude journal, and make a habit of writing down at least ten things every day that you are thankful for. Express thanks to the people you've met, the opportunities that have come your way, the challenges you've faced, your family members, and for whatever else you are grateful. In fact, I would like you to do it right now. Write down at least ten things you are thankful for in the space provided below. Begin your sentence with "I am grateful and thank you for…"

Write down ten things you feel thankful for:

1. I am grateful and thank you for _______________________

2. _______________________

3. _______________________

4. _______________________

5. _______________________

6. _______________________

7. _______________________

8. _______________________

9. _______________________

10. _______________________

How do you feel? If you do the above exercise sincerely, you will feel the positive energy inside you. Your energy will shift immediately when you are mentally in a state of gratitude. But don't take my word for it. Go and do it. Get a gratitude journal for yourself, and practice this every night before you go to sleep or first thing in the morning. You will feel the energy shift and all the good things on their way to you. Imagine how powerful your day will be if you begin your morning by expressing what you are thankful for, even if some days that's as simple as being thankful to be alive.

Cause and Effect

When your state of mind is in gratitude mode, you can understand and master this principle of cause and effect easily. As we've discussed, whatever is happening to you now is because of your past deeds. Therefore, if you don't like what you are achieving or getting now, you can't blame people or your environment. Instead, work on changing your mindset, your thinking, your feelings, and thus your actions.

You don't have to go to a fortune teller and ask what your future is going to look like. All you have to do is focus on doing the right things and carrying out the right actions that will bring you closer to your goals.

The challenge for many people who do not understand this principle is they don't make conscious choices and actions. They just react. They act when they are angry or when they are upset or worried. How often do you see people react immediately without giving themselves space to think and respond with an appropriate action?

You need to understand that this principle of *cause and effect* applies both to an individual and a business organization. What people within the organization do today has a great impact on the results they are going to get in the future. Therefore, as the business owner or leader in your company, you need to be able to make conscious choices. You need to think of the consequences that will arise from the choices you make and decide on appropriate actions before jumping to a conclusion without proper consideration. Don't act or make decisions purely based on stress, fear, worry, or anger. Consider instead making data- and fact-driven decisions.

In November 2018, I decided to attend a five-day seminar in Toronto, Canada, conducted by Bob Proctor, a world-renowned speaker, motivational coach, and the author of many best-selling books. I am so grateful that I made that learning trip because it's had a great impact on my life since then. At the seminar, we received a unique coin from Bob. The coin has two sides, one with a smooth surface that has a beautiful phrase printed on it: "Respond and You're In Control." The other side is rough and has the sentence "React and You Lose Control." I love this, and I always carry it with me. Whenever I'm facing difficult times or challenges, I just rub my fingers over the coin. As I touch the smooth surface, it reminds me to respond to the situation and not react.

When you *react* to the things that are happening to you, you do not give yourself space to cool down and make conscious choices. You just react based on your emotions. This reaction means that you are not taking control; your emotions are taking control of you. When you respond to things that are happening to you, you will notice and be aware of your emotions. You'll be able to take a step back, give yourself space, and allow yourself to think and make conscious choices. As such, you will be taking control of your emotions and mastering your life. You'll think before you act!

Summary

Live your life to your fullest potential. Hold the steering wheel and don't allow situations, circumstances, and people to affect your thinking, feelings, actions, and goals. Be the master of your life.

Here are three ways you can begin immediately to make changes that can have a great impact on your life, your performance, and your business:

- Commit to giving and sharing something with everyone you meet with no expectations of reciprocity. Ask yourself:

How can I bring more happiness to people around me?

How can I help more people?

How can I make more people successful?

How can I help my customers?

How can I help my suppliers, my team?

- Start or end your day by thinking of things you are thankful for. Write them down in your gratitude journal.

- When facing challenges, practice responding consciously rather than reacting emotionally. Give yourself some space and time to settle down and think. Accept things as they are, knowing that they're happening because of your past actions. Focus on doing what is right now, and firmly believe that things will get better soon and that you can weather all challenges in your life because you are the master of your own life.

CHAPTER 4

ALIGN THE PROCESSES

A well-aligned and connected process is capable of producing more consistent and high-quality outputs with fewer resources at a faster speed.
– Casey Ang

As mentioned in chapter 2, well-designed and connected processes yield higher output, giving you higher revenue and profits. On the other hand, a poorly designed and disconnected process can cause unnecessary waiting times, delays, and other inefficiencies. This increases headcounts and costs and may severely affect the revenue and profits of your business in the long run.

In this chapter, we'll focus on aligning processes for better connectivity to achieve higher effectiveness and efficiency in fulfilling customer orders.

First, let's discuss some of the common symptoms of disconnected processes. You may want to go through the following list and check how many of them happen in your organization.

- Unplanned stoppages or delays in the process are due to lacking information or data.

- High frequency of reworks or looping back to earlier steps is due to error or quality issues.

- People are working around the clock but do not seem to be able to meet the demand.

- A discrepancy in meeting customer expectations is often detected only at the last minute when a product or service is about to be delivered or is being delivered.

- People work without clarity about their priorities.

- Work is jammed in between processes for unknown reasons.

- A high percentage of employees are missing deadlines.

- People feel exhausted and have low morale.

- Problems are pushed from one department to another without being resolved.

- People fix the process bit by bit as problems pop up and get caught up in "fire-fighting" mode.

The list goes on, but these are some of the common symptoms I always look for when I am visiting my consulting client's company. Are any of these symptoms familiar to your company?

I hope by now, you can see how important it is for you to get your process aligned. The time you invest in establishing a well-aligned and connected process can help prepare your business to face upcoming economic challenges as well as allow your business to weather COVID-19 and other unexpected events.

What Is a Process?

A process is a series of tasks and activities that take place to convert inputs to the desired output. As shown in figure 4.1, the inputs are being converted to the desired output by going through a process.

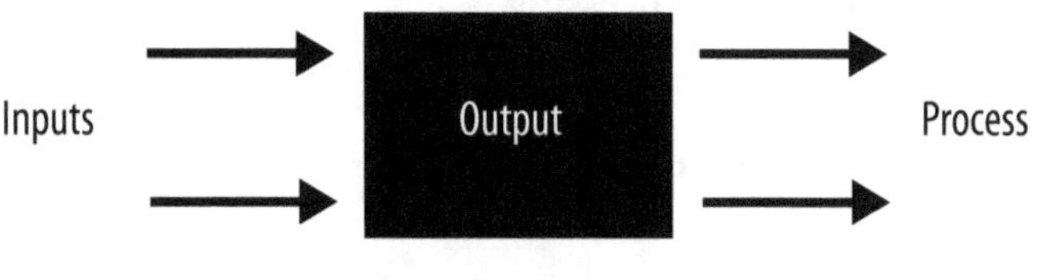

Figure 4.1

If you zoom into the black box process, you will see a series of activities involved in producing the final output. As illustrated in figure 4.2, you see that the output from a previous process (left circle) becomes the input to the next process until the final desired output (right circle) is produced.

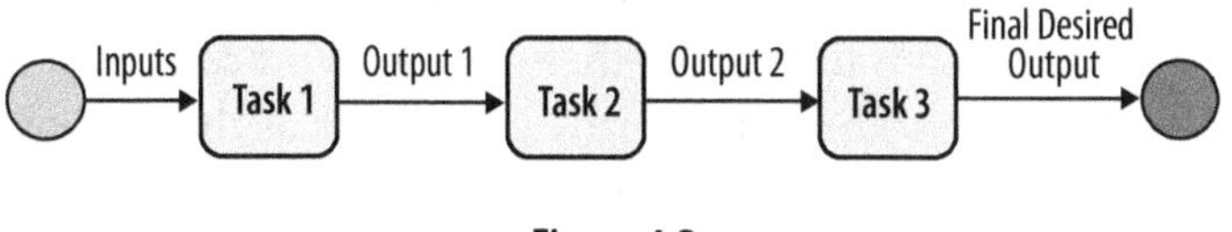

Figure 4.2

A well-aligned and connected process means the following:

- The expectations between the inputs and outputs from each task within the process are clearly defined and clear to all task owners in the process.

- Each task owner clearly understands the duration for completing the task and what level of quality they must produce to create an input for the next task in the process.

- All tasks can be executed with few interruptions and without a stoppage from the beginning of the process to the end.

- People working on each task get to see clearly what is coming to them and how they should prioritize their work.

Here are some examples of processes within a business organization:

- Customer order processing
- Issuing job orders
- Planning and scheduling
- Procurement
- Production
- Customer service

In the rest of this chapter, I will explain the seven steps that you can take to align and connect your processes.

Seven Steps to Align and Connect Processes

1. Map the Overall End-to-End Process

The first step is to map out the end-to-end process. What is an end-to-end process? This means charting out all the processes involved in generating revenue and profit for the company. Depending on your industry or type of business, you need to identify the end-to-end process and make sure that it is well aligned and connected. The following table provides some examples of end-to-end processes for certain types of business.

Nature of Business	End-to-End Process Scope
Manufacturing	From receiving the order until the order is shipped and payment collected
Retail	From displaying the product until the customer pays at the counter
Café and Restaurant	From greeting customers until the customer pays the bill
Project Based	From receiving an inquiry or request for tender (supply of goods or services) until the project is completed and payment is received

Mapping out the high-level, end-to-end process allows you to understand the relationship between the processes involved in fulfilling customer orders. I will not explain in detail here about how to map the process, but you may visit my website (www.casey-ang.com/resources) to access free resources on how to map the business process.

You may notice that the end-to-end process does not include other shared services functions, such as:

- Human Resources

- Information Technology/Management Information Systems (IT/MIS)

- Finance

- Corporate Communications

These are also important functions in making sure the end-to-end processes, and thus the business, can operate at the optimum level of performance.

My recommendation is to start with the end-to-end process and focus on getting these processes aligned and connected. As you follow the seven steps discussed here, you will also identify the essential supports required from the shared services functions. You can then further align with the related supporting shared services functions.

2. Identify the Producing and Enabling Processes

Once you have the end-to-end process map ready, the next step is to identify and classify producing and enabling processes. *Producing processes* are involved directly in making the final product or providing the service, whereas *enabling processes* provide essential support, materials, and information to the producing process. The main role of the enabling process is to ensure the producing process is able to run at its optimum performance with fewer interruptions and stoppages due to inaccuracies, delayed materials, lack of information, and other issues.

The concept here is to ensure that we remove all the unnecessary burdens to the producing process and that we make sure it is always optimized to provide what the customer wants at the right time, in the right quantity, and with excellent quality.

How do you differentiate between producing and enabling processes?

Producing processes are those processes that when they have problems, they directly impact the product or service you sell to your customer. Without producing processes, you would have no product or service. Enabling processes assist the producing processes by providing necessary resources, infrastructure, and supports but do not directly result in the final product or service.

The table below provides examples of producing and enabling processes for certain types of business. Please note this is not an exhaustive list, and the processes might be slightly different in your company. My intention is to give you some examples so that you understand the difference between producing processes and enabling processes.

Nature of Business	Producing Process	Enabling Process
Manufacturing	Research and development (R&D) (if available) and production	Production planning, procurement, warehouse, quality inspection, logistics
Retail	Product life cycle management	Procurement, customer service, merchandising, warehouse, logistics
Café and Restaurant	Cooking food	Customer service, procurement, cleaning and facility maintenance
Interior Design	Designing spaces	Handling inquiries and quotes, project scheduling and management

3. Set Expectations

Your next step is to set clear expectations for each process and to make these expectations known to all the people involved. This step is important, so make sure you involve all the relevant process owners and stakeholders. Take time to drill into the details and align the expectations between processes.

Start with defining the expectations and requirements regarding the output from the producing process. Ask these questions about the final product or service to customers:

- How long should it take to produce the final output?
- What is considered an acceptable level of quality to the customers?
- From a business perspective, what is the total capacity of the process required to meet the demand?
- How much revenue and profit should be generated from each product or service category?
- What is the acceptable profit margin performance for each category of product or service?
- What are the specific inputs or supports required from the enabling processes? Spell out the details in terms of what is required, when they are required, and how they will be provided to the producing process.

Next, work on the other interrelated processes within the end-to-end process and set specific requirements and expectations between them. Ask these questions:

- What is the expected cycle time or duration for each process?
- What are the downstream processes? And what are their expectations in terms of what is required, when it is required, and how it will be provided?
- What is considered an acceptable level of quality for the outputs from each process?

- Where and how should the outputs from each process be sent?
- In which areas between processes are projects designated as pending, and what is the maximum allowable number of projects that can be pending?
- How are you going to identify and track the status of work in the end-to-end process?
- How can you make the status visible to all the relevant people in the end-to-end process?
- What guidelines should everyone follow in setting the work priority?

As you list the expectations between processes, you may identify some conflicting interests as well as some misalignment. It is good to let those misalignments surface and to get the related functional team to discuss and align them. The goal is to improve the ability of the company to provide what the customer wants, when they want it, with the right quantity and quality, at the right price to the customer, and at a profitable margin for the company.

4. Set Clear Roles and Responsibilities

Define clear roles and responsibilities for each task in the end-to-end process. The aim is to eliminate any gray areas of responsibility or, as I call it, "no man's land." What do I mean? A gray area or "no man's land" refers to a process step that confuses people because no one is sure who is responsible for ensuring the task is carried out properly and that it meets the expectations established in step 3. The result of this confusion is that work is pushed from one area to another without anyone really looking into it because everyone thinks, "Someone is responsible for it, but not me."

Therefore, it is important for you to scrutinize every task and make sure the roles and responsibilities are defined clearly for each process. This includes defining the expected level of performance for the person responsible for carrying out a task. The person in charge of the task needs to know what is expected of him. For example, what is the expected service level? What is the expected throughput per day? How fast should the work be completed? What are other related performance indicators?

You also need to define a method for measuring the key performance indicators so that the task owner knows how they can contribute to move the indicator in the correct direction.

5. Define What Initiates the Process

Next, define the signal that initiates each process. In other words, you want to make sure all the people responsible for the tasks know *when* they should start working. This is particularly important for processes that are not physically located next to each other. Unlike a continuous flow production line where each step is linked by conveyor belt, such that the person next in line has to pick up the work that flows in, work on it, and complete it before the next one flows in. In the situation where the related processes are separated in different locations, then a clear starting signal must be defined to ensure that all projects can flow through smoothly from beginning to end.

This can be done by setting a clear dependency between the tasks. For example, task 2 must start when task 1 is finished; such a relationship is referred to as Finish to Start in project management. Or the relationship can be Start to Start; for example, task 4 must start when task 3 starts. In some workflow or project management software, you can set the task dependencies easily, and the software will send notifications to the task assignee based on the dependencies set.

I also find it useful to set a specific location, be it a physical location or a specific shared folder in your computer, where all the incoming work will be placed. A clear identification or label can be used to indicate the sequence of projects coming in, and guidelines can be set as First in First Out (FIFO), where the person in charge works on the task that comes in first.

Classification of tasks by urgency or priority can be another way to allow the task assignee to know what to work on first. For example, if any tasks are in the High Priority or Urgent area, then they must be addressed immediately upon arrival. However, you need to make sure that people follow the expectations set in step 3 in terms of setting priority; otherwise, you may get into a situation where everyone starts labeling their tasks as Urgent and demanding immediate attention.

6. Identify Potential Disconnects

By now, you have already mapped the overall end-to-end process, identified the producing and enabling processes, established clear expectations and requirements among each process, set clear roles and responsibilities with measurable performance indicators for each process, and defined a clear signal to initiate each task in the process.

The sixth step involves examining the process for any disconnects and addressing them. Here are five symptoms to look for.

    a. Gaps: Walk through the process and identify areas where there is incomplete data or information. Look for symptoms where the process stops due to waiting for information or data. Address these gaps and update the process expectation set in step 3.

    b. Redundancies: Look for redundancies, places where projects are looping back to previous steps for reworking or correction. Identify the high rework or re-loop area, fix the root cause, and reduce or eliminate the need for rework. Also, look for redundant data entry or redundant approval signatures. Question the value of each step by asking appropriate questions, such as: "Do we really have to do this? Why do we have to fill out three forms to get one thing done? Do we really require all five department heads to approve this?"

c. **Unclear Customer Requirements:** Do you have a high internal reject rate? Are these rejects genuine or because of a lack of understanding of customer requirements? What about customer complaints? Are the producing processes being fed with accurate customer requirements? Do you see symptoms where processes are being slowed down, or where resources are being added to perform tasks people assume are important to customers, but that are not aligned with actual customer requirements?

d. **Conflicting Objectives:** Identify areas where there are conflicting objectives. This is especially true when it involves cross-functional roles. For example, if the only key performance indicator (KPI) given to the procurement department is lowering costs, and the cost is the main driver used in evaluating and selecting suppliers, what may happen? While we expect the production department to be able to complete the production process fast, they are often given a poor-quality incoming part that causes delays. Also, check whether you have given the right tools and equipment to people working on the task. Sometimes I see companies not providing the correct jig or tools to the workers and yet complaining about their inefficiency. Employees have to waste time searching for a tool or waiting for a tool because it is shared and is not available when it is required. The same applies to office work—sometimes, people who are required to deal with lots of data are given slower laptops, which causes unnecessary delays.

e. Unclear Hand-Offs: This should be minimized if step 4 is being carried out appropriately. Look for the "no man's land" or gray area as described in step 4. Redefine the responsibilities of this area and make sure they are known to all the related stakeholders.

7. Simplify and Automate

Finally, work on simplifying the process. Look for opportunities where you can reduce unnecessary steps. Identify areas that require complex manual effort and seek opportunities to automate these whenever you can. For example, if the operator must assemble two parts by manually holding the parts and tightening eight nuts with a manual screwdriver, then think about creating a holding jig and having them use an electric torque control screwdriver. Aim for those high-repetition areas and find ways to simplify and automate them. For instance, a simple MS Excel macro program may reduce the time it takes to compile regular reports from hours to a few seconds with just a few clicks.

Summary

The time and effort you spend working through the seven steps discussed in this chapter are certainly worthwhile. It may feel tedious for you and your team, but once these steps are done, and with continuous improvement, it will boost the productivity, efficiency, and effectiveness of your organization by many times compared to what you are achieving today.

Pull your team together and work through all seven steps. As illustrated in figure 4.3, this is not just a one-time effort; it is a cycle of continuously improving the process to ensure it's always aligned and able to support and respond to the changes in your business's strategic direction as well as changes in the market.

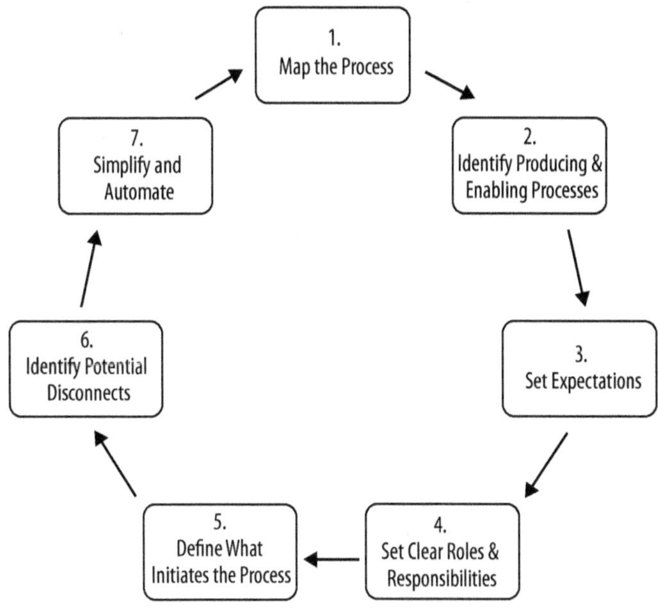

Figure 4.3

SET
CLEAR
GOALS

CHAPTER 5

OVERCOME MENTAL HINDRANCES

To accomplish great things, we must not only act, but also dream; not only plan but also believe.
– Anatole France

Have you ever set a goal for yourself?

Whenever I ask people attending my seminars to set a goal, I always like to see how they respond. Generally, I see two patterns. Group one becomes uncertain about what goal they should set. Group two gets into it immediately, as though they have already thought about it and know what they want. Whenever I have a chance, I always like to probe group one; without fail, I always find out they do have a goal. Deep inside them, there is something they want to achieve, but they lack the self-confidence and faith to put it down on paper. They worry that if they write it down and don't achieve it, people will judge them.

Fear of failure and *fear of rejection* are the two major mental hindrances that you must overcome if you ever want to achieve something big, something you want deep inside your heart.

The rest of this chapter explains the techniques to overcome these hindrances.

Your Natural Instincts

If you can, go back to the time when you were just a baby. You will realize that at that age, you had no fear of rejection and failure. You knew what you wanted, and you would do whatever you could to get it. If you were hungry, you'd cry until you were fed. When you started to learn how to crawl, walk, run, talk, you set a goal in your mind of what you wanted to do, and you kept trying. When you fell, you cried because it hurt, but you never gave up because that was your goal. You had no fear of failure and rejection. You did not care how people looked at you or responded to you. You just did what you wanted to do with pure intention and persistence.

Where have all these instincts gone in your adult life? You see, it's been natural for you to set goals and achieve what you want since the day you were born. As you grew up, you started to hear judgments about your capabilities. Subconsciously, you started to understand what you are capable of and not capable of. A high percentage of people convince themselves that not being able to do what they truly love is okay. They start to tell themselves, "I have to be realistic. Maybe one day, when I have X, then I will do it." You and I both know they'll never do whatever it is they long to do.

Isn't that sad! I believe life is not just about earning a living, not just about earning money. Money is just a material symbol. Many people give up what they truly love to do because they believe that they don't have enough money to do it. They may love to travel, but they worry if they travel, then they won't have enough money. They love music, but they feel they do not have enough time to learn music because they need to work hard to earn a living.

Is there something you'd absolutely love to do that you haven't started yet?

The Higher Purpose in Your Life

Everything I've learned about goals, I've learned through experience. As I am writing this book, I'm approaching fifty. It's because I listened to my heart and believed that I could do what I love to do that I became a business consultant. I am also grateful to have met another longtime goal of mine, which was to become an author. From a young age, I always loved to share my knowledge and what I know with people. I love teaching. Whenever I share something, there is a feeling of satisfaction in my heart. I know that teaching is my calling in this life. I believe there is talent in me that I can use to help people be successful, and I enjoy doing that more than anything else.

Because of my goals, I grab opportunities that allow me to share my knowledge and inspire people to do more and achieve more. I tried to set up my own consulting business and failed. I went back to work at a company for a while after I failed. But deep in my heart, I knew what I wanted, and I knew failure was just making me stronger and smarter. And in December 2018, I tendered my resignation from a well-paid, senior management position and pursued my dream one more time. Now, I am writing this book, and I've created a consultation and training company, Lenoxcells Sdn Bhd (www.lenoxcells.com). It has been a very exciting journey. I know I am on the right track now, and the sky is the limit. I am sharing this not to impress you but to impress upon you that you, too, can achieve the goal that you set.

Having a goal gives us a sense of purpose in life. It gives us the energy and passion for living up to our fullest potential. A person without a goal is like a ship in the middle of the ocean without a destination, just letting the currents dictate its direction. A life without a goal is a life without a purpose. In fact, a person without a goal or a sense of purpose may become depressed or old before their time. I am sure you have come across people who do not know what to do after they retire. Life is suddenly blank to them, waking up in the morning without any purpose to pursue. They are likely to age faster than goal-oriented people, and their health may deteriorate prematurely.

Focus on What You Want

Your job is to get clear in terms of what you want and to focus on whatever that is. You do not have to worry about how you are going to achieve it when you set a goal. Because when you become truly clear and firm in what you want, then the how will become apparent. Everything around us starts from a clear intention and an idea in someone's mind before it manifests in the physical world. The satellite TV in our house, the smartphone, the laptop, the car, the airplane, even the social media platform we use—they all started from a thought, an idea, in the mind. Just like the greatest inventors, you also have the ability to tap into unlimited creative power.

Remember, when you are not going forward, you are going backward. The world is getting smaller; things are changing and moving faster. The only constant in this world is change. If you are not growing, you are shrinking. Setting a goal that you truly want but do not know how to achieve can make you uncomfortable and insecure. But it is this feeling of discomfort that leads to growth. You've probably heard the analogy that if you put a frog in a pot of boiling water, it will jump out immediately. But if you put the frog into nice warm room-temperature water and gradually heat it up, the frog will die in the water because by the time it realizes the water is too hot, it can't jump anymore.

This story also relates to setting a goal and getting out of your comfort zone. When you get stuck for too long in your comfort zone, your creative muscle starts to shrink, and you stop learning and acquiring new skills. Suddenly, if a crisis comes and forces you out of your comfort zone, you may just collapse and not know what to do. Bob Proctor, a master of personal development, says that goals keep us moving and growing and have moved humans from living in caves to condominiums. He also says that "setting a goal makes you a better person, parent and professional."

Aim High and Be Persistent

When it comes to setting a goal, aim high and be persistent. Set a goal that you want strongly in your heart, that excites you and keeps you moving forward. It may also scare you because you have no clue how to accomplish it. A goal like this facilitates growth and keeps you going despite challenges and obstacles.

Ask yourself, what do you want to achieve? What is the one thing that you love to do? Go ahead, write it down now. Get clear in terms of what you want and firmly believe that the how will become apparent as you focus and move toward your goal. Keep moving; be persistent. Thomas Edison said he didn't fail 10,000 times; he just successfully discovered 10,000 ways that didn't work. As documented in their biographies, many great achievers share certain characteristics: they set clear goals and were persistent in pursuing them. Not only did they set goals and try to achieve them, but they also visualized themselves achieving them. They acted, spoke, and walked as though their goals had already become their reality.

Obstacles and Challenges Make You Stronger

Obstacles and challenges you'll face when pursuing your goal can only make you stronger and smarter. They will not stop you from achieving your goal unless you give up. Someone who has not experienced failure simply means he has not tried moving beyond his comfort zone. You have a choice: you can believe your goal is attainable, or you can believe it's unattainable. Why choose to believe it's unattainable? There is nothing you cannot achieve if you set a clear goal and never give up.

Enjoy the process of pursuing your goal. Become aware that achieving your goal is not your only objective—the journey is where your growth happens. If you set a goal with a journey state of mind, I can assure you, you will love it. It becomes so self-fulfilling to wake up in the morning knowing that you're going to take action to move closer to your goal, knowing that you will learn, grow, and improve along the way. Isn't life beautiful? You are pursuing your goal but not becoming attached to the results. Focus on your goal, keep working toward it, searching for solutions, and see if you can imagine yourself already achieving it. You will start to attract the people, situations, and opportunities that will help you get closer to your goal.

Goal Card

I am so grateful to Bob Proctor, who introduced the Goal Card concept to me when I was in Canada in November 2018, attending his five-day seminar. Since then, I always carry the Goal Card with me. One of the goals I wrote on my Goal Card was to write a book—and well, here we are. I want to give all credit to Bob Proctor and the Proctor Gallagher Institute for creating this Goal Card. You can find your own Goal Card at the end of this book. Cut it out or copy it, write your goal on it, and put it in a plastic sleeve so that you can carry it with you. Read it as many times as possible each day. When you touch the card, it will remind you about your goal and make you feel excited about achieving it. I know it works because it's worked for me.

Summary

Here are the key points from this chapter:

- The desire to set and achieve goals is something you're born with. Ever since you were a baby, you have been setting goals and achieving them.

- You must overcome your fear of failure and rejection if you want to achieve something big, something meaningful in your life.

- Setting goals gives your life a purpose. It inspires you and gives you the energy and enthusiasm to live up to your fullest potential.

- Focus on what you want—get clear on it. The *how* will become clear along the way. Tap into your unlimited creative power.

- When you are not going forward, you are going backward. Setting goals pushes you out of your comfort zone and enables you to grow.

- Aim high and be persistent. Believe that you can achieve what you determine to do. You will only fail when you stop or give up.

- Obstacles and challenges you'll face when pursuing your goal only make you stronger and smarter.

- Choose to believe you can achieve your goal, and you will notice things start to fall into place for you. You will start to attract people, situations, and things that will move you closer to your goals.

- Enjoy the process of pursuing your goal. Embrace the journey and notice how it facilitates your growth.

- Use the Goal Card at the back of this book. Carry it with you. Write your goal down and read it as many times as possible each day. Visualize achieving your goal when you touch the card.

Successful business entrepreneurs have clear goals. They set a clear direction for their company. They know where they are leading the company and have full confidence that they will get there. In the next chapter, I will discuss the process of setting clear goals for your business.

Before you flip to the next chapter, *make sure you write down your goal on the Goal Card*. Enjoy the process of setting and pursuing your goal. Give yourself a pat on your shoulder and tell yourself, "I am growing, improving, and advancing every day."

CHAPTER 6

SETTING THE DIRECTION AND GOALS FOR YOUR BUSINESS

*Persist and persevere, and you will
find most things that are attainable, possible.*
– Bob Proctor

*The real leader has no need to lead—he is
content to point the way.*
- Henry Miller

Successful entrepreneurs have strong faith in themselves. They often have a vision in their minds and then work step by step to turn their vision into reality. Walt Disney saw Disneyland in his mind before building it. In fact, he passed away before Walt Disney World launched in Florida in 1971. He never got to see the theme park in person, but he had already seen it in his mind, and this is why we can see Walt Disney World today.

Jack Ma, the founder of e-commerce giant Alibaba, saw an opportunity when he was first introduced to the internet in

1995 when he visited the US. He started Alibaba after persuading seventeen of his friends to invest and join in. He tried so many times to raise funding from venture capitalists, but they all rejected him. Many people thought Alibaba was a bad business model, but he believed it was going to be big. In fact, for the first few years, they had no revenue. But he kept moving forward. Today Alibaba is one of the world's largest e-commerce companies, and Ma also owns Taobao, Tmall, and Alipay.

Behind every successful business, there must be a great leader—a leader who has a great sense of direction and who knows where he is leading the company. A leader has a clear vision and can persuade others to come together to build the company. A company led by this type of leader will go far and be able to weather challenges in the business world. They may be defeated in the market, but they will make a comeback and become even stronger. They will keep learning, growing, equipping themselves with stronger capabilities, and keeping themselves up to date with the latest developments in their industry. Because of this, they're often able to differentiate their company from others in the market.

You might have heard the saying, "Without vision, people perish." The same goes for a business organization: companies who do not have a clear vision of the future often struggle to attract and retain the right talent. They fail to let the people working in the company know the direction of the company, the vision, and mission. People are not certain about where they will be in three to five years. As discussed in chapter 5, a person without a goal lacks a sense of purpose. People who get sucked into a company's daily operational issues and challenges feel tired and exhausted at the end of the day because they do not know where they are heading or why. Companies like this often fail to grow—that is, if they're even able to launch in the first place.

Think big and set a big goal! People always love to be part of a team that creates magnificent results. They feel proud to be part of it. The goals may seem impossible initially, but if a leader holds the vision firmly and has complete faith, they'll be able to persuade people to come along. Although the journey won't always be smooth and requires effort and time, people enjoy knowing that they are working toward a bigger goal. They share a common vision. It is this common vision that brings team members with different backgrounds together to pursue something bigger.

Have the guts to be different. What is the mission and vision of your company? What are the milestones that the company needs to achieve to move closer to its vision? From the financial aspect, how much improvement do you need to see in terms of revenue and profit? Is there a new segment of the market you would like to reach? Do you need to improve time to market for your new product? How successful have your sales and marketing strategies been so far? Start to think of areas of improvement or goals that your business needs to achieve. These can be short term one-year goals, or they can be long term, such as three-to-five-year goals, or you might even have a ten-year vision.

As the leader in your company, you need to think about ways to free yourself up from day-to-day operational matters. This action is crucial so that you have more time to invest in developing the market, setting strategies for your company, and meeting new customers. You must be able to create a structural system that enables your team to take care of day-to-day operational matters with minimum dependency on you. Therefore, as you are setting the goals for the business, also look into the essential training you need to provide, operational systems you need to establish, and what technology you can adopt to ensure the company can operate effectively and efficiently.

How should you set goals for your business? Here are seven steps.

1. Reflect

The first step is to reflect on your business's current situation and achievements. Here are some important objectives:

- Identify current strengths, weaknesses, opportunities, and threats.

- Build awareness of changes, trends, and opportunities you can tap into or potential challenges you need to be aware of in the micro environment and the macro environment.

- Gain a good understanding of your year-to-year progress.

- Compare the performance between cross-functional departments.

- Benchmark your company's performance against other players in the industry.

Knowing where your company stands is a crucial step in setting goals. Checking the facts and data allows you to compare your company's reality with your assumptions. Sometimes I see an organization rely on a subjective claim, such as "Our customers are happy with our service," or "We are fulfilling all our customer orders on time." These claims might have been true in the past, but when you scrutinize real performance data, it may tell a different story. Therefore, unless you check the facts and data, the goals you set may not be relevant and won't address crucial issues.

2. Set the Stage

If you carry out step one well, you will identify areas that you need to focus on and work on. The second step is to set the stage. This means creating a sense of urgency for people in your organization about why there must be a change in those areas. Doing this will enable you to pull the team together so that everyone is on the same page and able to see the importance of acting immediately. This unity helps you to set the stage right before you determine your goal. People are generally more willing to participate and accept challenges to strive for a higher goal when they understand the urgency and reason for the change.

3. Set the Goals

You need to be aware that your organization has limited resources; as such, the focus is to ensure all resources are channeled effectively and efficiently toward fulfilling the most important goals of the business. It is important that you not be too ambitious and set too many goals at one time because it will diffuse your team's focus and lead to superficial solutions.

I would recommend three to five goals at one time. Think systematically and identify your primary goal in a few different sectors: Financial, Business Development/Customer Relations, Internal Operations, and Human Resources.

Make sure the goal you set has specific timelines and is measurable. As the old saying goes, what gets measured gets done.

At the same time, also make sure the goal you set challenges your team to grow. Think big. Set a goal based on what the business needs. Major breakthroughs will excite everyone. The goal is to be able to put the company in a better position in the market and accelerate its success and growth.

4. Communicate

Once the goals are set, make sure you communicate them to people in the organization. Communicating goals does not mean merely announcing them and saying, in essence, "These are the goals, now go achieve them." You need to make sure they understand the goals, and more importantly, they understand how they can contribute to the goals. For example, if one of the goals is to achieve at least 98 percent on-time delivery performance, then there are some important things you need to address when communicating this goal:

- How are you going to measure on-time delivery? Is it based on the date we commit to the customers or on the date the customer wants it?

- Who is responsible for measuring and tracking this performance? How will it be communicated to stakeholders?

- Why is the target 98 percent?

- How can each person in the company be involved in fulfilling orders in a way that contributes to achieving this goal? If it's not communicated well, people may just look to the production team to take the lead on this goal. In fact, it's a company-wide effort: the planning team needs to be able to work closely with procurement to ensure production is able to get the parts on time; the warehouse needs to be able to kit the material on time for production to use; incoming quality control (QC) needs to inspect the parts correctly to make sure only good parts are supplied to production.

5. Empower the Team

People are the soul of an organization. They are the asset. If you take care of the people, they will take care of the business. Invest in developing your people's capabilities in a way that's aligned with the business's directions and goals; this is crucial, and the returns are always magnificent. Empower your people by giving them the right tools and equipment, the freedom to speak their minds, and even the courage to make mistakes and face failures. In an organization, you have people coming from different backgrounds with different experiences and qualifications. Some of them may have been with the company since day one, and some may be newcomers. When combined, they form a Team Paradigm. This means the collective beliefs they have about the company and about what they think they are capable of and not capable of.

A few years back, I was called into a local SME company to help them to reduce the lead time of their internal operation. After listening to the requirements and plant tour, I suggested an in-depth on-site analysis to understand the root causes of long lead times and how to overcome them. But the team, comprised of leads from various departments, shared with me that they were not sure I would be able to help because they had tried everything they could think of for years, and nothing had worked. This is a typical example of a Team Paradigm. In response to their doubts, I asked them, "If all of you, as the leads in this company, think that there is nothing much you can do to improve the lead time further, then what will your team think about it?" In asking this, I shook up their paradigm and pulled their focus to why they thought they needed to reduce the lead time in the first place. I was awarded the project, and together with the team, we managed to not only reduce the lead time, but to double the output.

In pursuing the goals you have set for the business, you need to address the Team Paradigm. One of the ways to do this is by raising the team's awareness of their true potential. The other thing I have found useful is to get the team to understand the reason for a change, to help them feel a sense of urgency, and to help them focus on what they can do instead of what they cannot. Again, when the *what* and *why* are clear, the *how* will become apparent.

6. Celebrate Small Wins

Look for small wins. Celebrate and recognize your team's efforts and contributions. This helps to shift their paradigm and reinforce the new belief that if they pull together, they can achieve more. Remember, the journey to a goal leads to tremendous growth. Recognizing your team's efforts will inspire them and give them the motivation and energy to continue the journey. Each time you do this, you are reinforcing the new belief and shaking their old paradigm. As a consultant, I always like to spend time talking to the people who are performing the work. Sometimes when I talk to them, I hear things like, "No matter what we do, the boss will always say that is not good enough," or "Our boss doesn't understand what we did, and we don't understand why." You know, the people who are doing the work are normal human beings who have emotions, and they need attention and recognition from time to time. You will be surprised at their response and the results they deliver if you get into the habit of praising good work.

7. Be Persistent

Take my word for it: in pursuing your goals, you will encounter many challenges and obstacles. Some of these you can take care of, and some will continue to dog you. *Persistence is the only answer.*

Press harder and keep searching for a solution until the goal is achieved. Be flexible; look for another solution if what you have tried so far does not bring you the results you want. Hold firmly to what you want to achieve for your business, but don't be attached to the results you get. Because when you become attached to the results, your emotional self takes charge. You become worried, stressed, and lose faith about whether the goal you set is achievable.

When you can remain unattached to results, you keep your mind calm and focus on your goal. Your desire to achieve that goal must be so strong that you can already envision attaining it. Nothing will steer you away from achieving your goals; your mind will always keep seeking out solutions. As Jack Ma says, "Never give up. Today is hard, tomorrow will be worse, but the day after tomorrow will be sunshine."

Summary

To achieve BIG results in your business, you need to have a pool of talented people in your organization. To attract the right talents to your organization, you need to have a clear sense of purpose and direction for your company. People always love to be part of the team that creates magnificent results. Follow the seven steps given in this chapter, and start setting goals for your business.

ENGAGE

AND EXCEL

CHAPTER 7

HOW TO FULLY ENGAGE IN EVERYTHING YOU DO

To achieve great results, you have to be physically fit, mentally aligned, emotionally calm, and spiritually inspired.
– Casey Ang

By now, you are ready to excel and to accelerate in all aspects of your personal life and business. The key to fully engaging is managing your energy. This capability will be the focus of this chapter.

Manage Your Energy and Tasks

Let's start by discussing time management. I've found over the years that most people seem to think that if they can just manage their time, they can manage everything on their plate. I used to think that way as well. But over the years, I've started to realize that it is not about the time. After all, we all have twenty-four hours in a day. *It is about managing your energy and your tasks.* You need to be able to spend your time productively in the activities related to your goals. You need to focus on *20 percent* of the activities that will yield *80 percent* of your results. When it comes to fully engaging, less really is more. This is why I mentioned in chapter 6 that you need to stick to three to five business goals at any one time.

We are living in a digital world and race through our lives without asking the true purpose of our lives and what we really want to achieve. What do you really want to achieve? I hope by now, you have already set a clear goal for yourself as well as for your business. If you have not done so, I urge you to do it now. *Take the Goal Card in the back of the book and write down your goals.* Having a clear idea of where you want to be is the key to fully engaging. Without it, you are going to drift, and you'll waste a lot of energy in the process.

Tap into Unlimited Creative Power

Pursuing your goals doesn't have to be hard. You can achieve anything you want in your life if you know how to tap into the unlimited creative power in your subconscious mind. Using that power, you'll master the art of fully engaging in what you are doing.

Holding a belief that things must be improved gradually, one step at a time, over a period of time, is a *limiting paradigm.* As such, you need to focus on what you need to achieve, regardless of your current capability. Focusing on what you really want instead of what you think you can do puts you in a different headspace. Yes, it may seem scary and impossible, but when you think about achieving it, you'll feel so proud of yourself and excited about your accomplishments. This is the kind of energy that will move you closer to your goals. Shift your paradigm: aim high, aim big. That will keep you engaged during the whole journey of pursuing your goals.

Create a New Habit of Thinking

Next, create a habit of thinking and acting in a way that

enables you to fully engage in doing what you need to do to carry out your goal. For example, before you start working on anything, ask yourself how much time you think you should spend on this task. Set a time limit, focus, and get into it. Shut down all sources of interruptions. *Focus on one task at a time.* When you are working on the task, make sure your mind focuses on it as well. Do not think about other things on your plate or worry about something you don't need to do yet. Doing so will only diffuse your energy and extend the time and effort you must spend on the task at hand. So, practice this habit: if the task should only take one hour to complete, do not spend more than that. Avoid being too perfectionistic. Spend that one hour, and get the first output out. If you are not happy with it for whatever reason, then you can always revisit it later and fine-tune.

Focus on the Present Moment

Practice staying in the present moment. Your ability to stay in the present moment is the best gift you can ever give yourself. Train your mind to focus on one thing. Do what you need to do and have faith that the unlimited creative power in your subconscious mind will guide you to the right path. Let go of your attachments to the results. Do not struggle with the results you are getting now. That is not your job. Your job is to focus on what you want, believe that you are attaining it, fully engage in working on the solutions, and let go of any attachment to the results.

Worry and doubt will only drain your energy and reduce your ability to focus and engage. A mind that is full of doubts, worry, fear, and stress is like an ocean with strong waves. If you throw a big stone into rough seas, you won't see anything happen. But if you drop a grain of sand into still waters, you'll see the ripples immediately. When your mind is in a state of calm, peace, and confidence, and when you feel inspired and motivated, your intention is communicated clearly and immediately to your subconscious mind, and transformation begins.

Practice Effortlessness

When you master the art of working with the unlimited creative power in your subconscious mind, you start to notice the meaning of effortlessness, or what Dr. Joseph Murphy refers to as Easy Does It. Murphy suggests that the principal reasons for failure are lacking confidence and believing that success is only possible through hard work.

The more you study and understand how the mind works, the better you can connect to your inner self, the source of unlimited power and ideas. This connection enables you to channel all your conscious focus on what you want. When you can engage in what you are doing with that effortless state of mind, lots of ideas surface. I strongly believe that an organization should create this awareness in its people. Just imagine the results that the company can achieve if everyone in the organization can clearly see the vision they are pursuing, have faith, feel a connection to their subconscious mind, and fully engage in the actions they take to work toward a goal.

Step into the Field of Uncertainty

Learning to enjoy and live with uncertainty is another way to fully engage in what you are doing. As human beings, we naturally dislike uncertainty because it makes us feel uncomfortable. We like to work on something with minimum risk or more certainty because it gives us a feeling of comfort. However, if you do not learn to live with uncertainty, then it is going to be challenging for you to stay engaged in pursuing your goals. Because when you are working on something you really want but are not sure how to achieve it, you immediately step into the zone of uncertainty. Just imagine, if you want to do something but hesitate because of your capability, you are taking one step forward and probably two steps backward. Your mind is always asking, is this the right thing to do, what if you fail, what if this happens, and so on. So how can you focus?

Accept uncertainty. You'll be surprised when you do. Imagine you're on vacation. If you just follow the itinerary the travel agent gives you, you're sure to see some good scenery and have some good meals. But sometimes, when you veer off the beaten path, you're pleasantly surprised by the unexpected. Have you ever had this experience? Remember, you can only be certain about things that have already happened. So, when you notice you are in the zone of uncertainty, congratulate yourself because you are exploring something new, and in doing so, you are working toward your goal. Learning to enjoy living with uncertainty helps to remove unnecessary turbulence in your mind and allows you to engage physically, mentally, emotionally, and spiritually.

Add Enthusiasm and Passion

Fall in love with what you are doing. Enthusiasm and passion will keep you engaged in working toward your goal despite the challenges and obstacles in front of you. When you create a burning desire for your goal in your heart, it's easy to do what you need to do to get closer to it. You'll enter a flow state, where you're so immersed in what you're doing, you don't even notice the time passing.

Develop Healthy Habits

Support your commitment to engagement and working toward your goal by practicing healthy habits. Eat a balanced diet, exercise regularly, and drink enough water each day to stay fit and healthy. Build good sleep habits, and consider going to sleep early so you can wake up early. Spend time in nature and connect to the abundant sources of positive energy you find there. Rest when you feel tired.

Summary

Remember these tips to stay engaged:

- Focus on 20 percent of the activities that yield 80 percent of results.

- Write your goals on the Goal Card. Having a clear goal is essential to engagement. Without one, you'll drift.

- Pursuing your goals doesn't need to feel hard.

- Shift your paradigm: aim high, aim big.

- Set clear time limits for yourself when approaching tasks.

- Practice staying in the present moment.

- Tap into the unlimited creative power of your subconscious mind and notice what feels effortless.

- Learn to be okay with uncertainty.

- Fall in love with what you are doing.

- Learn to live a healthy and balanced life and maintain good physical fitness and health.

CHAPTER 8

DIGITALIZE BUSINESS PROCESS

*If you can complete a task in just a few steps, never
settle for doing it in over ten steps or more.
Keep looking for opportunities to simplify your process.*
– Casey Ang

In his research paper, "Digital Transformation and the Race Against Digital Darwinism," Brian Solis describes digital transformation as a realignment of business models, technology, and processes that can add new value for employees and customers. He called this the era of digital Darwinism and points out that organizations struggle to evolve at the same rate as technology and society.[1]

In thinking about making your business more resilient in the face of challenges, it's important to consider how you can digitalize your business processes. In this chapter, I'll offer some tips to help you tap into the benefits of process digitalization, specifically data automation, creating a digital interface, and connectivity.

---

1. Source: www.briansolis.com/2014/09/digital-transformation-race-digital-darwinism

Benefits of Digitalizing of Business Process

Digitalization can impact organizational performance in major ways. It provides opportunities for a company to enhance its competitiveness in the market, improve its operational effectiveness, increase efficiency, and create new business opportunities.

In their research paper, Klaus North, Nekane Aramburu and Oswaldo Jose Lorenzo shared:[2]

> The Boston Consulting Group (BCG, 2013) surveyed the IT adoption of more than 4,000 SMEs in Germany, China, India and Brazil. They found that leaders in technology adoption created jobs almost twice as fast as other SMEs and their annual revenues grew faster than firms with a lower level of technology adoption.

In the same paper, they also identified the main reasons for SMEs wanting to embrace the digital economy: internal efficiencies, cost reductions, better collaboration, and the ability to offer new products and services.

So how can digitalizing your business process improve internal efficiencies? First, let's look at data automation, which means applying suitable process technology, equipment, or systems to collect, analyze, and store data obtained from digital devices such as bar code readers and radio frequency identification (RFID) readers. In short, this looks like collecting process data at its point of origin via a digital interface.

Data automation helps eliminate the need for manual data entry in operational processes. As such, people running the process can free up their time to focus more on value-adding activities. Data automation also helps improve data accuracy by eliminating human error in manual data entry.

---

2. Source: www.emerald.com/insight/content/doi/10.1108/JEIM-04-2019-0103/full/html

Because the data can be collected instantly at its point of origin, the people running the process can monitor the process performance on a real-time basis and take appropriate corrective action before defective parts or products are produced.

Data automation has transformed information-handling tasks, such as during the checkout process in a store, in the inventory process in supermarkets and warehouses, and elsewhere. It makes information more reliable, faster to share, and easier to capture.

In chapter 2, we discussed Visualization. It is crucial for you to establish a visual dashboard that organizes, stores, and displays important information from multiple sources into one easy to access location. A dashboard enables you to monitor your business and operation performance in a timely manner. This can be done by connecting devices, sensors, controllers, protocols, interfaces, machines, I/O modules, gateways, and data transmission infrastructure to databases and data lakes that store and analyze the extracted data. You can see the output of such an analysis in various forms, including charts and tables that can be displayed on an LCD monitor in strategic locations at the company. The ability to see your data visualized is almost as valuable as having the data in the first place.

With the insights data automation provides from your downstream process, you can act proactively. The results of your data analysis process can feed artificial intelligence processing to the upstream process. Through this, the process parameters in your upstream process can be optimized via automatic and real-time adjustments and fine-tuning based on the outputs from the downstream process.

For example, in my work with clients, I've used V-One[3] software, which collects big data from a cloud server database

---

3. https://www.v-one.my/

such as enterprise resource planning (ERP) or a point of sales system for analysis. It enables us to provide fully flexible visualization drill-down charts and effective dashboards that provide meaningful insights to my clients in real time. Visit my company website (www.lenoxcells.com) for more information and examples of how to apply and benefit from data automation and a digital visual dashboard.

In chapter 2, we discussed the importance of a well-connected process in supporting the strategic growth of your business. Connectivity means all the work can flow from beginning to end seamlessly without unnecessary stoppages due to employees waiting for information or materials. People running the process have clear expectations of one another, and they know what and when to provide materials and information. They know the expected timeframe to complete their tasks. They also know the level of quality they are responsible for delivering.

Connecting your business processes through the use of a digital workflow management platform like Wrike, which I've used often, allows you to link the process together with an almost 100 percent paperless operation. A job can be initiated in this digital platform, and all related tasks will be automatically assigned to pre-sets based on the standard business process and workflow. This integration helps improve efficiency immediately, whereby people downstream are immediately triggered to start their work upon completion of a prior task. In addition, all the related documents or checklists related to the task can be unified in this digital platform. This helps to reduce unnecessary emails as people no longer have to chase down documents or information required to perform the task. A digital workflow platform like the one I am using even allows review and approval by all stakeholders—all in the same platform. The beauty of doing this is that you do not have to get someone to walk around in the office to get approval signatures.

It is time for organizations to rethink whether it is necessary to own a big office space just to keep everybody together to facilitate work. In my opinion, the era of digitalization creates opportunities for companies to reassess the concept of working remotely. People can work from anywhere so long as the business processes are connected digitally. If you need a meeting, people can just jump into any number of online meeting and conference solutions such as WebEx, Zoom, or Ding Talk. During the COVID-19 crisis, companies have had to shut down their in-office operations to keep employees safe. Imagine what's happened to those companies that have not digitized their work process. The work cannot be carried out. People are not able to work from home if processes are not established and connected digitally.

Adapting to new technology is not a choice when it comes to your business—it's a must. To improve the ability of your business to respond to sudden changes and crises in the macro environment, you will most likely need to digitalize your operations.

Guidelines for Digitalizing the Business Process

The challenge for many SMEs is where and how to start. Don't just jump into process digitalization for the sake of doing it without a clearly defined set of objectives and implementation strategies.

In the research paper "A Conceptual Cooperative Model Designed for Processes, Digitalization and Innovation," Daniel Sehlin, Maja Truedsson, and Peter Cronemyr write:[4]

> There is still no known way to systematically connect different kinds of processes and innovation activities with a well-defined methodology. To access the right technical knowledge can be difficult, especially for Small

---

4. Source: www.emerald.com/insight/content/doi/10.1108/IJQSS-02-2019-0028/full/html

and Medium Enterprises (SMEs). Hence, there is an opportunity for SMEs to digitalize business processes with the expertise of an external party.

So, here's how to get started digitalizing your business process:

1. *Define the objectives.* What's most important to your business with regards to process digitalization? What are the key improvements you want to see from it? This is critical because too often, I see organizations struggling to adopt technology because they either did not define business objectives at the outset, or their objectives shifted. Consequently, a digital platform, rather than simplifying their process, actually complicates it.

2. *Establish a well-aligned process.* Attempting to digitalize your current processes without streamlining them is a dangerous and costly mistake that many organizations have made. As discussed in chapter 4, you first need to align and simplify your business process before you attempt to digitalize it. Follow the seven steps suggested in chapter 4 to make sure your business processes are well aligned and connected.

3. *Identify the highest-potential process.* Do not attempt to change things overnight. The process of digitalization is a journey that must be planned and executed well. Start from the highest-potential process. To do this, clarify your producing and enabling processes, as discussed in chapter 4. Focus on the areas with pressing needs, for example, where there is too much manual information transmission and multiple manual data entry happening. Streamline the process, remove redundant steps, and digitalize it with a suitable workflow management platform, such as Wrike.

4. *Understand customer demands.* Find a way to meet those demands in new and innovative ways through a digital platform. For example, identify the step in the process where customer input or approval is required before work can continue. Connecting this area with your customer by using a digital workflow platform enables your customer to receive notifications instantly. An appropriate digital visual dashboard also can be made available to your customers, so they receive updates about their projects and orders in real time. This improves communication with customers, and it helps to build trust and brings more orders to your company.

5. *Develop new capabilities and responsibilities.* As you undergo the process of streamlining and digitalizing the business process, expect changes in roles and responsibilities. When less or no manual data input is required, human resources are freed up. Take this opportunity to provide new training and skills and move employees into areas that add more value. If this is not planned well, you may meet strong resistance to change, or people might try to complicate a simple process just because they still think the process needs them to be there, and they worry about what's going to happen to them if this process is simplified and digitalized.

6. *Evaluate long-term benefits versus short-term costs.* Sometimes I see companies, particularly SMEs, who hesitate to invest in a cost-effective solution because of the immediate cost of implementation. I think being cost-sensitive is important, but a company must also understand the return on investment they can get from process digitalization. Consider the many hidden costs of disconnected and inefficient systems. Consider how many people it takes to

enter data manually and move documents from one place to another. Consider how much time is lost in gathering and analyzing information. These are just some of the examples of hidden costs. So think long term; the short-term investment you make not only cuts down on hidden costs but also opens up more opportunities in terms of higher sales and a better reputation, hence winning your company more new customers.

7. *Get help from outside experts.* The world is getting smaller, and information and help are available at your fingertips. Don't overlook resources you could use to help your company digitalize the business process. Enlisting an expert or consultant can bring in new ideas and inspiration, and hence improve your company's internal capabilities. Speed is the answer in today's competitive and fast-changing business environment. You may take many years to do it yourself gradually, but your competitor could be leveraging resources right now to optimize their operations.

Summary

The only constant in this world is *change*. There are already many cost-effective process digitalization solutions available in the market. Make a commitment to be more proactive in searching for the one that is suitable for your business. Follow the seven steps discussed in this chapter to start digitalizing the business process. Remember, the main objective is to make the technology serve the people who are running the process and not the other way around.

R.I.S.E. MINDSET™

Achieving excellence in business and your personal life means having the right mindset. This mindset forms the foundation for all your other efforts. Without it, no amount of training, resources, or tools will make a difference.

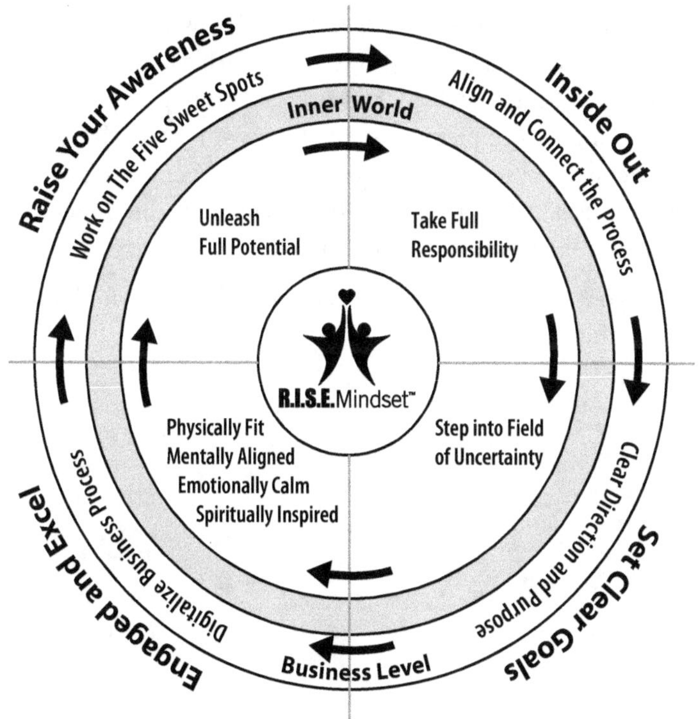

Embrace a R.I.S.E. Mindset™. Commit to following this process and watch the effectiveness and productivity of your business double. Remember these points:

1. If you know how to tap into your true potential and the power of your subconscious, you can achieve excellent results easier and more effectively. So focus on your inner well-being first, and notice how this begins to shape what happens in your outer world.

2. Balancing a profitable business with a fulfilling life is not just a dream. If you follow what we've discussed in this book and create a system that enables your people to run the business effectively, with less dependency on you, you'll find more freedom and satisfaction.

You'll never know your true potential, what you're truly capable of achieving, until you stop wondering and start doing, so start putting the R.I.S.E. Mindset™ into practice today. Embracing and implementing it starts with internalizing the basic concepts, setting clear goals, and fully engaging as you strive to attain them. It's true that change can be difficult at first—but the rewards will be worth it.

So go for it! Here's to your success, and thank you for joining me on this journey.

GOAL CARD

<table>
<tr>
<td>

I am happy and grateful now that:

____
____
____
____
____

Having a goal gives us a sense of
purpose in our life.

A person without a goal is like a ship in the middle of the ocean without a destination, just letting the currents dictate its direction.

Casey Ang

</td>
<td>

I am happy and grateful now that:

____
____
____
____
____

Having a goal gives us a sense of
purpose in our life.

A person without a goal is like a ship in the middle of the ocean without a destination, just letting the currents dictate its direction.

Casey Ang

</td>
</tr>
<tr>
<td>

I am happy and grateful now that:

____
____
____
____
____

Having a goal gives us a sense of
purpose in our life.

A person without a goal is like a ship in the middle of the ocean without a destination, just letting the currents dictate its direction.

Casey Ang

</td>
<td>

I am happy and grateful now that:

____
____
____
____
____

Having a goal gives us a sense of
purpose in our life.

A person without a goal is like a ship in the middle of the ocean without a destination, just letting the currents dictate its direction.

Casey Ang

</td>
</tr>
</table>

R.I.S.E. MINDSET ™
COACHING FOR BUSINESS EXCELLENCE

R.I.S.E. Mindset™ Coaching for Business Excellence is a program I have put together to help business entrepreneurs uplift their business performance through the R.I.S.E. Mindset™ framework discussed in this book.

The approach of uplifting the business performance through embracing the R.I.S.E. Mindset™ will empower you and get you ready to lead your business to the next level of performance in a systematic, simple, and effective way. The following diagram illustrates the journey that we will go through together in this coaching program.

Four Milestones in the Journey of Transformation		Embracing R.I.S.E. Mindset™	Uplifting Business Performance
R	**R**aise Your Awareness	1. Gain clarity of your true potentiality – unleash your full potential	2. Set the fundamental in place – visibility, traceability, connectivity, productivity & capability
I	Inside Out	3. Taking charge of your own life	4. Realign and connect your process to increase productivity
S	**S**et Clear Goals	5. Overcome Mental Hindrances – Discover Your Natural Instincts	6. Set 1- to 3-year goals for your business
E	**E**ngage & Excel	7. Get Physically Fit, Mentally Aligned, Emotionally Calm and Spiritually Inspired to Excel	8. Establish a plan to digitalize the business process and watch the improvement in productivity & effectiveness at work

Please visit my website (www.casey-ang.com) to find out more about how you and your business can benefit from the R.I.S.E. Mindset™ Coaching for Business Excellence program.

ABOUT THE AUTHOR

A speaker, author, consultant, and coach, Casey Ang has delivered more than 1000 speeches and has coached more than 5000 individuals from various sizes of business organizations. Casey is an expert with 20 years of experience in building an effectively operating system for running a profitable business by blending business performance improvement skills with the R.I.S.E. Mindset™ framework.

Casey's areas of expertise include:

- Creating an effectively operating system to run a profitable business

- Inspiring people to perform up to their fullest potential

- Managing organizational change through the R.I.S.E. Mindset™ framework

- Improving productivity through process digitalization

- Inspiring happy organizational culture for high performance

With every donation, a voice will be given to the creativity that lies within the hearts of our children living with diverse challenges.

By making this difference, children that may not have been given the opportunity to have their Heart Heard will have the freedom to create beautiful works of art and musical creations.

Donate by visiting

HeartstobeHeard.com

We thank you.